MY TUMMY
IN CHURCH

CHRISTY COLBY HENO

Dimensions for Living

Nashville

MY TUMMY TALKED IN CHURCH TODAY

And 51 Other Humorous Poems and Devotions for Adults Who Love Children

ISBN 978-0-687-49011-0

07 08 09 10 11 12 13 14 15 16—10 9 8 7 6 5 4 3 2 1

Manufactured in the United States of America

To my mom and dad,
who showed me what love truly is,
and to all my friends
at St. Luke's United Methodist Church,
who listened and laughed at all the right times,
offering endless support.

CONTENTS

FOREWORD

Christy Heno is one of those rare and wonderful people who not only "lights up a room" when she walks in but also touches your heart with her radiant smile and winsome Christian spirit. You will find that dramatically in the warm pages of this book. Her positive outlook, her gracious theology, her keen insights into human nature, her amazing sense of humor, her special love for and understanding of children and her deep commitment to Christ, all come together here in a special way in these uplifting devotionals.

As you read her words in "My Tummy Talked in Church Today" and the other devotionals, you will be reminded that the word "Gospel" means "Good News," not bad news or harsh news or judgmental news or "holier-than-thou" news—no, it is the good news that God loves us more than we can imagine and God is reaching out to all God's children with "Amazing Grace" and "Unconditional Love."

Bright, upbeat, compassionate, perceptive, thoughtful, kind, loving, eloquent, tender, inspirational, Christy Heno is all of these and much, much more!

I had the unique privilege to work daily with Christy on the same church staff for several years, and I saw her live her faith in times of joy and sadness, in times of victory and challenge, in times of great accomplishments and in times of heart-wrenching grief. And in each and every one of those circumstances, her depth of faith, hope, and love radiated brightly and inspired all those around her. Now through this book her faith can reach out and touch others in a beautiful way.

I commend Christy Heno and her book to you highly! You will be blessed by her words and by her spirit!

Jim Moore

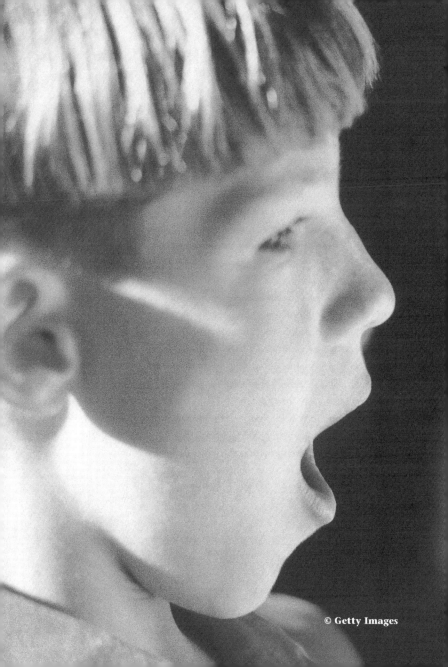

INTRODUCTION

A few years ago I had the privilege of helping bring an amazing performer to my daughter's elementary school. For his show, he acted out several poems by such poets as Shel Silverstein, Jack Prelutsky, and A. A. Milne. He totally captured the children and I could see through their smiles, the light in their eyes, and the laughter in the room that he had single-handedly brought poetry to life for these children. That very afternoon I took my two daughters to the bookstore and the first thing my six-year-old said was, "Where is the poetry section?" She was hooked. We left that day with two new poetry books and with every trip back to the bookstore, our collection grows.

Children love poetry. As a teacher I used it in my classroom to show children just how fun words can be, to teach them about the world around them, and most of all to encourage their love of reading. As a mom I use it to connect with my children and bring conversation and laughter into our days. As the director of children and family ministries, I began to notice that there are very few, if any, poetry books written about religion. Poetry that allows us to see church through the eyes of a child. Poetry that helps us bring our faith home and invites conversation with our children. Poetry that makes talking about our faith with our children fun. So, I started writing. What you have before you hopefully will bring joy and understanding to you and the children in your life. My hope is that you will read, laugh, discuss, and celebrate your faith with your children as you read these poems together.

Blessings to you all!
Christy

I'M GOING TO BIG CHURCH

I'm going to big church
With long pews and all
I'm going to big church
It's right down this hall
I'll hear lots of music
And say lots of prayers
I'm going to big church
I hope God is there.

But Jesus called for them and said, "Let the little children come to me, and do not stop them; for it is to such as these that the kingdom of God belongs."
Luke 18:16

Wow! Imagine what the sanctuary must look like to a child for the first time. The sheer size alone would be amazing and maybe a little scary. Then they sit down and notice the hymnals, the Bibles, and of course, those pencils just waiting to be used. Suddenly the music starts. Little hands cover little ears and their eyes grow as the choir starts to sing.

Can you imagine? Can you remember that feeling? To be so excited and in awe of everything? Why, it would be simply impossible to sit still when there is so much to see. Why, then, do we worry so when our children are showing

10

their excitement? Why do we feel the need to make these little spirits sit down and be absolutely silent? Why do we feel the need to take the "fun" out of church?

Now I am certainly not saying that we should let them run wild or yell and scream or stick their tongue out at the person behind them, but what if we answer all their questions in hushed whispers, snuggling close to share what we know? What if we let them bring paper and crayons and draw a picture of God or whatever they are feeling at that moment? What if we let them sing loud and proud even if they don't know the words and are way off-key?

Can you imagine? Can you see the smile on God's face as we welcome God's children into God's home? They are going to big church. Show them God is there.

Dear Heavenly Father,
Each day you give us an opportunity to share your love and your word with our children. Help us be reminded of the awe we felt the first time we went to "big church" as we share that experience with them. Let us welcome them, as they are, as your son, Jesus Christ, did so long ago.
Amen.

THE OTHER COMMANDMENT

My shoes are tight
My belt is snug
My hair's been combed just right.
My mom's had all my clothes laid out
Since six o'clock last night.
I'm brushed,
I'm fed,
My teeth are clean.
I've been inspected twice.
No dirty nails
No untamed curls
I've promised to be nice.
I have to get up early
When the sun can not be seen
But on Sundays before we go to church
My mom says,
"Thou shalt be clean."

God does not judge by external appearance.
Galatians 2:6 (NIV)

Appearances! Sometimes we can get so caught up in what
we look like or what someone else looks like that we
forget to look at the most important part of a person—the
heart. It is so easy to pass judgment based on a glance
rather than a word.

Why is that? How have we become so concerned about appearances?

One of my favorite things about children is their ability to see into a person. They seem instinctively to know if a person is kind or mean, playful or serious. They judge more on a smile, the sparkle in a person's eye, or the tenderness of their voice rather than the make of their handbag or their looks.

Think of the people you truly love. Now ask yourself, if their appearance or circumstances changed tomorrow, would you suddenly stop loving them? No, because the people you love are people you know from the inside out, not just from the outside. As you go through this week, try to get to know someone new who might not "look" like you. You might be pleasantly surprised by what you find inside them.

Dear God,
Thank you for the people in our lives. Help me to remember that we are all made in your image. Help me to look at others with the eyes of a child, with loving rather than judging eyes.
Amen.

THE BIBLE

So many words
Such little print
Did you know there are 66 books in it?
Genesis, Exodus, Deuteronomy, too.
Matthew and Mark to name a few.
With Psalms in the middle
And stories throughout
I'm ready to learn what it's all about.

The sum of your word is truth.
Psalm 119:160

I recently attended a small group discussion where we had to finish the sentence, "In my opinion the Bible is. . . ." Maybe you can relate to some of the answers: "God's Word," "long and hard to read," "sometimes scary," "full of great stories," "inspirational," "a guideline for our lives."

No matter how you see it, the Bible is an important part of our faith. And yet, so many of us are overwhelmed by the idea of reading it. If we struggle with how to read and interpret the Word of God, imagine what it must be like for children. Fortunately you can find great "beginner" Bibles for children, but it still remains up us to make sure our children truly understand the stories they are hearing and know the significance of the Bible. Helping our children

14

make real-life connections with the stories is critical to their understanding. If we don't make those connections, the Bible is nothing but a really long storybook in their eyes. And, as we help our children become more comfortable with the Bible, we may just find ourselves feeling the same way.

Dear Lord,
Thank you for the gift of your Word. Help us to find time each day to read your words and be comforted.
Amen.

UP IN FRONT

Everyone's so serious
Sitting up in front
No smiles, no laughs, no waves hello
Sitting up in front
I wonder who they're looking at
Or even what they think
But sitting up in front I think
Must really, really stink.

Worship the LORD with gladness.
Psalm 100:2

I always worry when I attend a worship service at a church and the people who are leading it have the most stern expressions on their faces. Once I overheard a child ask why the people in the front seemed so sad.

Now I know this is not the case in all churches, but I think it is a good reminder that our faces often show our emotions and we need to ask ourselves, "Does my face match my true feelings?"

I would venture to say that even those leaders who are looking sad or maybe even bored may actually be enjoying the service but are unaware that their body language is just not conveying that message.

Some people think that you should always be serious in service; and while I do believe that we need to be thoughtful and respectful when in the presence of God, isn't being in God's presence one of the most joyful experiences of all?

I certainly hope my children think so. When we have the opportunity to worship with others, to share in God's presence, I hope that we are moved to show joy with our faces and let everyone know that indeed, God is here and we are happy!

Dear Lord,
Thank you for your daily presence in our lives. Let us reflect to others the joy you bring to us.
Amen.

JEALOUS

I get sick of my brother
I really do
So when I heard Joseph's story
I knew it was true

Being jealous is easy
When your brother gets a cool gift
It can make you so mad
Though it gives him a lift

But I still can't believe
They were angry enough
To beat him and sell him
And all that mean stuff

I mean when I get mad or jealous
I might slam my door
Call my brother a name
But not really much more

But Joseph's brothers were harsh
They acted out in anger
And when you do that
There is sure to be danger

God tells us each day
Not to be jealous or cruel
It's a shame Joseph's brothers
Couldn't have learned that in Sunday School.

My Tummy Talked in Church Today

So his brothers were jealous of him, but his father kept the matter in mind.

Love one another as yourself. Thou shalt not be envious. Be ye kind one to another. How many different ways do we get the message, and yet that little green monster called jealousy always seems to find its way into our brains?

It starts early, even with toddlers. Have you ever watched toddlers on the playground? When they see something a friend has, they want it and will simply march right up and take it. As they get older, we hear ourselves saying many times a day, "Share!" Even as they hit elementary school, everything must be fair in their world, and when it is not, beware.

Still, hopefully we can help our children understand the importance of sharing and teach them to handle their emotions when things aren't going their way. It is hard in an age where people seem to feel entitled to everything—many times expecting something for nothing. It is up to us to help our children learn to count their blessings, to appreciate each day God gives us, and to, indeed, love one another.

Dear Lord,
Each day you fill our lives with more blessings than we can count. Please help us keep our eyes and hearts open to receive them.
Amen.

Humorous Poems and Devotions for Adults Who Love Children   19

MY TUMMY TALKED IN CHURCH TODAY

I didn't know it was coming
That sound from way below
I didn't know it was coming
It started near my toes
I wish I had eaten breakfast
Or brought a snack at least
But the rumbling kept on coming
Like some sneaky growling beast
I held my breath
And swallowed hard
I knew it was coming then
My tummy talked in church today
Thank goodness it said, "Amen."

He has filled the hungry with good things.
Luke 1:53

Why is it that we tend to push the hunger envelope? By that I mean why do we wait until our mood is so bad and we have snapped at everyone in our path, especially the children around us, to finally get something to eat? Low blood sugar is one of the fastest growing excuses for bad behavior out there today. "He's just tired" or "She missed her nap" are no longer the number one excuses. We are hungry!

Ron Benedict

In our family, we have even taken to making sure we have a box of snack bars in the car at all times in case somebody hits the hunger wall while en route somewhere. It can get really ugly.

But I am wondering, is it food we are hungry for? Is that the reason we see more frowns than smiles these days? Perhaps what we are really hungry for is that feeling of fullness that comes with our relationship with God. Maybe it is not our stomachs that need filling but our hearts. If we could all remember to take a moment each day to connect with God, whether through prayer, song, meditation, reading the Bible, showing kindness, or anything, maybe those "hunger" pains would go away.

It's worth a try and hey, maybe it will save you a little on your grocery bill.

Dear Father,
Thank you for the opportunities we have every day to refuel with your love. Help us remember to take moments each day to feed our spiritual hunger pains.
Amen.

My Tummy Talked in Church Today

OPEN OR CLOSED?

In a circle
Holding hands
Getting ready to pray
Everyone bowed their heads at once
But I don't pray that way
I like to keep my eyes wide open
And look around the room
I like to see the praying faces
I watch them 'til we're through
Some say that you should close your eyes
They think it's like a rule
But I don't think God really cares
He just wants to hear from you.

One of his disciples said to him, "Lord, teach us to pray, as John taught his disciples."

Luke 11:1

At the end of staff meetings in a church where I worked, we always held hands and someone would close our meeting with a prayer. When I am praying, I tend to look around sometimes, taking in the faces of my friends while listening to the prayer. One day one of my fellow staff members caught my eye during the prayer as he was doing the same thing. We made a silly face at each other and then immediately bowed our heads suddenly feeling like little kids who might get in trouble. We laughed about it later and talked about whether or not there is a "rule" about praying.

This of course led me to do a very unscientific survey and ask more of my friends what they did and what they thought. It was so fun to hear their responses. Most would laugh at the question because quite honestly it was not something they had ever considered. Some kept their eyes open but didn't really look around. Some did something different depending on where they were and what they were praying about. Still others had very strong feelings. To them you absolutely had to close your eyes and bow your head out of respect.

It's funny isn't it—how we all come to prayer in different ways? And yet, I cannot help feeling that God is just simply happy to hear from us and is not up there taking notes on who peeked. Because I believe in the end, God is hearing what is in our hearts no matter what direction we may be looking.

Dearest God,
Thank you for always hearing us when we come to you whether with eyes closed or open. Help us hear your answers in our hearts.
Amen.

My Tummy Talked in Church Today

BOWLING IN HEAVEN

"She's not ready for bowling yet,"
I heard my daughter say
As we talked about a girl she knew
Who had suddenly passed away.

I looked at her a moment
Confused but then to me it came
You see, in a six-year-old's eyes
Thunder and lightning are just one big game.

"What does she have to do," I asked,
To play with God and the angels this way?"
"Mommy, she has to pass a test
Or celebrate her next birthday."

"Guess what?" I said, "I've got good news.
Her birthday is next week.
She'll get to bowl with the angels
Sooner than you think!"

Take care that you do not despise one of these little ones; for,
I tell you, in heaven their angels continually see the face of
my Father in Heaven.

Matthew 18:10

Talking to children about death is a conversation that no one wants to have. We naturally want to protect our children from the sadness and suffering associated with death. Mistakenly, we use words like *lost* or *passed away* instead of stating the fact that a loved one has died and is simply not coming back. It may be a parent, grandparent, friend, aunt, uncle, brother, sister, or even a pet that has died, but the message remains the same. Someone special is gone and they are not coming back.

I have had this conversation with my children four times already, and their ages are not even in the double digits. Each time it has been me who has received comfort from them and their views of death. Each time I am reminded just how spiritual children are and how much closer they must be to God and true understanding than we could ever be. I love the idea that in the past my children have viewed Heaven as a place where their grandmothers play checkers with God and that another friend has apparently joined Heaven's bowling team. I love that they see death as a continuation of life and have found a way for it to make sense to them. I know as they grow older these ideas will change and lose that "magical" quality, but for now it gives me comfort to know that they see a loving God who clearly likes to have fun. Why, then, should anyone be afraid of death?

Dear Lord,
Death is a natural part of life. Thank you for greeting us with open arms and constant love.
Amen.

My Tummy Talked in Church Today

NAOMI TOLD RUTH

Naomi told Ruth to stay in Moab
But Ruth said, "I'll go with you."
Noah built a great big ark
And brought animals two by two.
David beat Goliath and
Esther's faith saw her through.
I love these stories,
They make me think
And wonder what I'll do.

But he said to them, "My mother and my brothers are those who hear the word of God and do it."
Luke 8:21

What inspires you? What makes you take that extra step to go into action and make a difference? Sometimes I find myself caught in what I call "idea" mode. I can come up with a lot of great ideas of things to do, businesses to start, classes to take, causes to support, and yet, a few weeks later that initial enthusiasm will be just a memory and those nagging doubts will have won again, telling me all the reasons each plan wouldn't work.

But what if Noah had given in to the doubts? Surely this man, asked to build an ark on sunny days to hold every animal, had his doubts. And what about David? Small in

stature, acting alone as he confronted the giant that was Goliath, surely he had doubts. Then we have Esther, risking her life for her people. Surely knowing death could be near would make you think twice before taking action, and yet, for Esther, it did not. All of these people relied on their great faith to see them through.

What great inspiration can we take from these stories? As we share them with our children, we have an opportunity to encourage our children to rely on their faith and take action. Let's encourage our children to get beyond the reasons why they can't do something and know the truth—that with great faith, anything is possible.

Dear Heavenly Father,
Each day we come face-to-face with many challenges and opportunities. Help us keep the faith and know that with you we can take action.
Amen.

MY FIRST COMMUNION

Take the bread, dip it in,
Pop it in your mouth.
It looked so easy
As I walked up
But now things are going south.
All I can think about
Are the words
That the preacher said,
"His body and blood
Given for you"
Keep floating through my head.
Now I'm feeling a little bit nervous.
My stomach is getting queasy.
I was so excited at first
Because it all looked so easy.
So I think I'll just keep thinking
That Jesus is a part of me.
I'm sure I'll get right through this.
Please say a prayer for me.

*Then he took a loaf of bread, and when he had given thanks,
he broke it and gave it to them, saying, "This is my body,
which is given for you. Do this in remembrance of me."*
                                                    Luke 22:19

There are some funny stories about the things children
do when they take Communion for the first time. I once

watched a child insist he wanted to take Communion with his family at Christmas. His mom agreed and up to the altar he went. I watched him take the wafer with a curious expression, and then dip it into the cup. So far, all was well. Then as my little friend put it in his mouth, things took a turn for the worse. His eyes grew large and panicked and he threw his hand over his mouth. His mother thankfully had kept an eye on him, and she swept into motion, grabbing him and racing out the side door. I wish I could tell you they made it outside, but I can't. The good news is the church was so crowded that very few people even saw what had happened, but I could not stop laughing. The look on his face was priceless.

It is easy to forget how strange Communion must seem to children. They are so literal about everything, and to wrap their minds around bread and wine being symbols of Jesus' body and blood could certainly be a bit unsettling. We need to remember that while things may make sense or seem completely natural to us, children see things in a whole different light. So I am thankful for that mother's patience and willingness to allow her child to be a part of one of the greatest and most meaningful rituals in the church. And I am pretty happy about her quick reflexes, too.

Gracious Lord,
Thank you for your Son and for the opportunity to bring our children closer to you through the rituals of our faith.
Amen.

A CHURCH'S YOUNGEST MEMBERS

A church's youngest members
Are quite a noisy bunch
They cry and yell at drop-off
And again when they want lunch

Some scoot and crawl or roll around
Some are cruising here and there
And most of these young members
Don't even wear underwear.

The smells, the noise, the diapers alone
Can cause one quite a scare
The church nursery is an amazing place . . .
I wouldn't step foot in there.

*And she gave birth to her firstborn son and wrapped him in
bands of cloth, and laid him in a manger.*
Luke 2:7

To watch a mother drop her baby off at the church nursery
for the first time can be absolutely heart-wrenching,
especially if the baby is her firstborn. I remember it well
myself. With a first child, mothers are absolutely certain
that no place in the world is clean enough or safe enough
for their child. They worry that the child care worker
won't understand exactly how to take care of their baby's

needs. No matter how much reassurance they receive, they still suffer when handing over their child. I have seen many mothers return to "just take a peek" only to make their little darling start to cry all over again.

When I think of how hard it is for us to let go of our children, my thoughts often turn to Mary. Can you imagine her putting her new baby in child care? Can you imagine her trusting anyone enough to watch over God's Son while she did some errands? What about when Jesus hit his teens? Was he difficult to handle at times? How do you ground the Son of God? And then ultimately, how did she watch that day as her son was put upon the cross?

As a mother myself, I can barely stand the thought. And yet, Mary did it. Mary had something we could all use a little more of every day. Faith. She had faith that things would be okay. She had faith in God. And she had faith in Jesus. She knew he had been brought to earth to do great things. She loved him and guided him and protected him, but in the end, she had to let go as all mothers do.

Loving God,
Thank you for your Son and for the precious children you bring into our lives. Help us cherish each moment we have with them and be willing to let go when the time comes.
Amen.

A WEE LITTLE MAN

I've heard about Zacchaeus
He was a little man
One day he couldn't see Jesus
So he came up with a plan

He climbed high into a tree
To see above the crowd
I'll bet that he was shocked
When his name was called out loud

See, no one really liked him
He was selfish and full of greed
But Jesus said, "Come on down"
For he saw a soul in need.

For the Son of Man came to seek out and to save the lost.
Luke 19:10

What a challenge Jesus places before us. He tells us to put others ahead of ourselves, to love one another. All throughout the Book of Luke, we see examples of Christ sharing his love with people we might cross the street to avoid.

Think of how the crowd reacted when Jesus told Zacchaeus he was going to his house. They were shocked that he was going to the home of a "sinner." They would never have visited with Zacchaeus in his home, and yet here was the Son of God doing just that.

What would you have done back then? What are we to do today? It's crystal clear. We are supposed to put others ahead of ourselves and love one another no matter how hard that may be.

What a valuable and yet sometimes difficult lesson we must teach children: that all of God's children are worthy of love. It is up to us to teach children kindness and tolerance and acceptance, and what better example to follow than that of Jesus?

Gracious God,
We thank you for loving us unconditionally and pray that each day we will recognize those in our path as people worthy of your love and ours.
Amen.

NEW CHURCH SHOES

Stiff and shiny
Brand spanking new
There is nothing
Like buying
A pair of church shoes.
They might
Have a buckle,
A snap,
Or some laces.
They always
Hurt your feet
In all the same places.
Mom says,
"Be patient
As you break them in."
I can't wait 'til
Next week
When I'll wear them again.

This is the LORD's doing; it is marvelous in our eyes.
Psalm 118:23

I had a friend who said you could always count on Jesus for a new pair of shoes. What she meant was that she always got excited when her "church" shoes were getting worn out because that meant soon her mom would take her to buy a brand-new pair. Her mother wouldn't allow her to wear anything but the nicest clothes to church, and worn-out shoes wouldn't do.

I always laugh when I think of that story and the idea of "counting on Jesus for a new pair of shoes." But it makes me think. Do we realize how much we can count on Jesus? Even as an adult it is hard for me to comprehend just what he did for us. I can't begin to imagine what was going through his mind as he faced the cross. What an incredible sacrifice for so many. He gave his life for us. With his actions he showed us we could always count on him.

I say let's try to live by that example. Let's try every day to be someone our children can count on; and let's show them this by our actions, with our words, and with our love.

Dear Lord,
How blessed we are to know we can always count on you.
Help us be there for the people in our lives and to show them
that they can count on us as well.
Amen.

UPON THE CROSS

He died upon the cross, they said
A crown of thorns placed on his head
I think of that a lot.

It started with Pilate's command
It's really hard to understand
I think of that a lot.

They said mean things, threw rocks and spat
Jesus forgave them even through that
I think of that a lot.

Upon the cross he died that day
Our sins were forgiven, washed away
I think of that a lot.

He rose again and everyone saw
That he gave his life to save us all
I think of that a lot.

Then Jesus, crying with a loud voice, said, "Father, into your hands I commend my spirit." Having said this, he breathed his last.

Luke 23:46

When I was little, I was always a little afraid when I saw a cross with Jesus on it. I had a Catholic grandmother, so there were several around her house, and I remember not really wanting to look at them because it looked so painful and kind of scary. As I grew older I got used to it, but still I never really thought about what it represented.

I know for young children, it would be really hard to understand what happened that day. My own children know Christ died for us. They even know that some mean people who didn't like him put him on the cross, but they don't know all the details. They don't know how Jesus was treated as he journeyed to the cross. They don't know exactly how he was put on the cross, or that his own mother watched. My girls would instantly ask, "Why didn't she help him?" It is too big for them to truly comprehend what was happening. To them, Jesus is the good guy, it doesn't make sense. Parents are supposed to protect their kids. Again, it just doesn't make sense.

Fully comprehending what was really happening and that it was all for us, is big. My hope is that as we teach our children our faith, we are careful with just how much detail we give them at each age. In the end, it is the love and joy of our faith we want them to know and to remember.

Dear God,
Please be with us as we share our faith with the children in our lives. Help us find the right words to share your story and your love. Amen.

EVERYONE CAME TO CHURCH

Everyone came to church today.
There was no room in the pews.
The aisles were full of chairs
Lined up in rows of two.
The balcony was overflowing.
The parking lot was full as well.
Everyone came to church today . . .
Easter sure is swell.

I want to know Christ and the power of his resurrection.
Philippians 3:10

While waiting in line to get into the sanctuary one Easter
morning I overheard a member say that he thought we
should have frequent visitor cards that get stamped each
time we come to church, and those with the most stamps
get in the front of the line on Easter Sunday. That led
another member to laughingly suggest the church should
issue fast passes, like they do at Disneyworld, for people
who regularly attend church and don't just come on
major holidays. That made us all laugh as we envisioned
people waving their fast passes as they dashed into the
sanctuary to get a good seat ahead of everyone else.

But it made me think. Shouldn't the very people who only
come once or twice a year be led straight to the front?

40

Shouldn't those who don't have a close relationship with God be brought in even closer to hear God's Word instead of being put in the back of the line?

If children are only going to church a few times a year, how can we expect them to have an understanding of who God and Jesus really are and the impact they can have on their lives? Yes, it can be frustrating for members not to get their regular seats on Easter Sunday, but think about the opportunity you may be giving a family to grow closer to God.

Generous God,
Help us remember that we are to share your Word as well as our seats in the sanctuary. Your doors are open to everyone and your blessings are a gift to each of us.
Amen.

LEFT OUT!

It started at my cousin's house
I couldn't believe my eyes
The sign on the door said
NO GIRLS ALLOWED!
Imagine my surprise.

The next thing I knew it was dinner
And time for the family meal
To the kid's table with you
All the moms said at once
And I thought, this can't be real.

Then later that day after dinner
I wanted to play in a game
But the big kids just said
You are too small
I was so angry I called them a name.

I felt so left out the entire day
I was feeling really mad
But I remembered a verse
That I heard at church
That made me feel really glad.

"Let the children come to me," said Jesus
That's what he said to do.
He wouldn't let anyone
Feel left out
Whether they were 1 or 92!

My Tummy Talked in Church Today

I am with you always, to the end of the age.
                                        Matthew 28:20

The stories in this poem were a part of a children's sermon I once did, and I was so surprised at how many adults came up to me afterward to tell me how much they could relate to it. It reminded me that everyone at some point in their life will experience that feeling of being left out. It doesn't matter if you are the most popular, the cutest, the funniest, the smartest, the most athletic, or even the most creative person or not. It is simply a fact that everyone will experience that feeling.

And it is at these particular times that we must remember we are never truly alone. God is with us every step of the way, loving us and holding us close. What comfort we can take in knowing God is there and what an important truth to teach our children so that they too never feel alone.

Dear God,
Thank you for always being near. How comforting to know you are simply a prayer away. Thank you for the courage you give us in those moments when we feel alone.
Amen.

FINDING JOY

Joy is finding a parking spot
Joy is finding a pew
Joy is hearing a message
That really means something to you.

Joy is hearing the music
Joy is saying a prayer
Joy is being forgiven
Knowing God is always there.

Joy is out there waiting
Joy is easy to see
Joy is about loving each other
And being a part of God's family.

*So the ransomed of the LORD shall return, and come to Zion
with singing; everlasting joy shall be upon their heads; they
shall obtain joy and gladness, and sorrow and sighing shall
flee away.*

Isaiah 51:11

Once I was involved in a church campaign promoting the
idea of "joy ahead." The idea was to help people see that
when we have a relationship with Christ, we will find joy.
We had stickers made, billboards put up, and commercials
aired to bring the message to as many people as we could.

Ron Benedict

It was uplifting just to see the words. Every day I would look at the sticker I had placed on my computer and think, yes, joy is ahead.

But then, as always happens in life, something happened. A member of our church staff family experienced a tragedy and for me and many, the joy was suddenly absent. In its place came all the *why*s and *how*s and *what's to come*s. We questioned how God could let things like this happen. We grieved together and held our friend up and waited for the pain to lessen. One afternoon during this time as I sat at my desk, I saw again the little "joy ahead" sticker. And at that moment, I realized that yes, there is joy ahead. I heard it in the laughter as stories were shared about the friend we had lost. I heard it in the comforting words everyone gave each other. I saw it through the beautiful flowers children made for the service, and I saw it in the strength God gave everyone and the great love that was shared.

Yes, life does have its ups and downs and there is simply nothing we can do about that. But if we teach our children that indeed, joy is ahead, and to hold on to that when the darkness comes, they will see that our Lord is with us every step of the way inviting us into the joy ahead.

Gracious Lord,
You give us great joy. During times of darkness, help us look
to the joy ahead and know that you are with us.
Amen.

5 + 2 = 5000

If your mother ever says "share"
And you think that it's not fair
Then listen to this
So you won't miss
The reason you shouldn't despair.

One day Jesus had come to town
Many people had gathered around
With the message complete
They wanted to eat
But not enough food could be found.

A boy had five loaves and two fish
Jesus said there's enough on his dish
Then he said a quick prayer
They all started to share
And everyone got their wish.

No one went hungry that day
And many started to pray
A little boy knew
Just what to do
That to share is Jesus' way.

Taking the five loaves and the two fish and looking up to heaven, he gave thanks and broke the loaves. Then he gave them to his disciples to set before the people. He also divided the two fish among them all. Mark 6:41 (NIV)

Share! How many times have you said that word to your children? I wish I had a dollar for every time I have said it over the years. I would retire tomorrow. When my children were younger, they would just look at me as if I had said something truly horrible to them and then reluctantly hand over whatever toy they had been fighting over. Now, I get the occasional eye roll and many reasons why they shouldn't have to share. They really like to argue their case now, but eventually they go ahead and share or else they know a lecture is coming. I love having Bible stories like the one above to share and discuss with my girls. What if that little boy hadn't been willing to share? What if instead he had stomped his feet and held tight to his dish? Everyone would have missed a miracle. All those people would have missed the opportunity to witness the generosity and power of Jesus.

As my children grow older I have noticed that they are beginning to understand the benefits of sharing—sharing with each other and sharing with those less fortunate. Hopefully someday *share* won't be such a bad word after all.

Generous God,
Teach us to share with generous hearts, remembering the example of your Son.
Amen.

THEE, THY, AND THOU

Why do they make it so hard
With thees, thys, and thous
Those words are really different
But we're supposed to know them somehow
Shall, shan't, and begot
Are a few more unusual words
Some of the words in the Bible
Are the strangest things I've ever heard.

You shall put these words of mine in your heart and soul, and you shall bind them as a sign on your hand, and fix them as an emblem on your forehead.
Deuteronomy 11:18

One of my favorite things about children is the way they can sing a song, say the pledge, or pray a prayer without actually knowing all the words. I love the confidence with which they just make up whatever they think fits. "Oh come all ye faithful, joyful and triumphant" quickly becomes "joyful and triangle." Or how about "Our father, Harold be thy name"? And my all-time favorite, which comes near the end of the pledge: "one nation, under God, invisible. . . ."

It is easy to forget that if we are reading from an adult version of the Bible with our children, there will be some explaining to do. Even simple words like *thou* don't automatically translate to *you* for most kids.

"Thy will be done"? No idea. That's where our patience and understanding must come in. Take the time to explain God's Word. Make sure the children in your life understand just what it is they are saying. Teach them that one word they are all sure to know is also found in the Bible. That word is love.

Understanding God,
You share your words of love with us. Help us help our
children make sense of your Word and understand most of
all that you love them.
Amen.

CHURCH MOUSE

You see him dart
From room to room
He thinks that you can't see him

He leaves a trail of
Donut crumbs
From the classroom to the gym

And when you happen
To catch his eye
He gives that great big smile

He'll hug your neck
Then off he goes
To roam the church aisle by aisle.

Even children make themselves known by their acts.
Proverbs 20:11

In every church, in every city or little town, there is one.
That one child you see everywhere on Sunday mornings.
It may be the P.K. (preacher's kid), or a child whose
parents are in the choir, or just a child whose parents are
very involved; and therefore they spend a lot of time at
the church. No matter what the case, this child knows
every inch of the building.

Ron Benedict

At our church I often see our "church mouse" with a cupful of donut holes taken from some unsuspecting classroom or maybe the youth loft. I have seen him speed across the front of the sanctuary right before a service only to go out the nearest door to continue his adventure. And while at first I worried greatly about his safety (and we have developed some checkpoints with him to ensure it), I also have to smile.

Can you imagine being so comfortable in a place that you want to see every inch of it and love spending time there? How wonderful that a child can feel so at home in God's house. As a parent I would be thrilled to know that my girls feel that safe and secure at church, knowing there is a friendly face around each corner and rooms filled with God's love.

Dear God,
Thank you for the church. Help us let the children in our lives know how happy we are to share your love and your house with them.
Amen.

My Tummy Talked in Church Today

IN CHARGE OF VBS

My mom's in charge of VBS
I think she's going mad
She keeps on mumbling numbers
And scribbling on a notepad

"10 boxes of this, 12 crates of that
Oh no, there's not enough glue,
Sequins, posters, or construction paper."
She cries, "What are we going to do?"

I'll be glad when VBS is over
And my mom's herself again
But until then she keeps on sending me
to count supplies again.

For we are what he has made us, created in Christ Jesus for good works, which God prepared beforehand to be our way of life.

Ephesians 2:10

I have seen grown women reduced to tears by glue bottles, or more specifically a lack of glue bottles. I have seen women guard a box of supplies with all the ferocity of a mother bear protecting her young. I have seen otherwise organized women lose all sense of direction and order and retrace their steps four or five times to the same supply room to get one more thing. Vacation Bible school. Sign up if you dare!

All joking aside, vacation Bible school is truly one of the most wonderful and meaningful weeks in the life of the church. What an awesome opportunity to share the Word of God with our children. Every year I am amazed at the dedication of volunteers, the number of hours spent preparing, and the enthusiasm they bring the first day after an exhausting week of getting ready.

Sometimes it is easy to lose sight of the big picture and why we do VBS. It is not about the T-shirts or the decorations or the snacks. It may not even necessarily be about the lessons we have prepared. It is about grown-ups being living examples of Christ to our children. It is about showing love and patience. It is about making each child realize that he or she is indeed special in God's eyes.

So take a minute this summer, especially if you are a part of the vacation Bible school machine, and ask yourself, "What are children seeing when they see me?"

Dear God,
We thank you for the opportunity to reach out and share your Word with children. Help us keep our focus on you.
Amen.

LIKE ME!

I snuck into the church today
It was as empty as could be
There wasn't anyone else in there
Which was a little scary to me.

I never really realized
Just how big a place it is
I called out my name, it echoed back
So then I yelled, "Gee whiz!"

Then back and forth I ran and ran
Going up and down the pews
I was really having a lot of fun
And it made me think of you.

I hope you had a best friend
And ran around and played
I hope you got to catch a fish
I'm pretty sure you prayed.

Maybe you were a lot like me
And thought of cool stuff to do
Maybe you snuck in a temple
And heard your echo, too.

The child grew and became strong, filled with wisdom; and the favor of God was upon him.   *Luke 2:40*

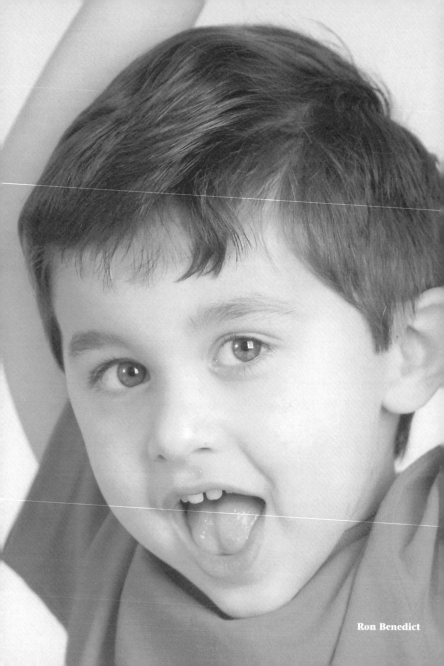
Ron Benedict

Have you ever wondered what Jesus was like as a little boy? Have you ever wondered if he always listened to Mary and Joseph or if he had chores or even if he had friends to play with?

I have. I wish there were passages in the Bible that told us more about Jesus' youth. I wish there was a way for children to identify with Jesus as someone "just like them" rather than see him only as another grown-up. How comforting it might be to a child to learn that Jesus got in trouble for not cleaning his room, too. Or that perhaps Jesus sometimes had trouble making friends because people thought he was different. (What with being the Son of God and all.) I want children to know that he understands the challenges they face on the playground and has felt the same happiness of winning a game or making a new friend.

I think it is important for us to help children understand that Jesus loves us because he was like us.

God,
Thank you for sending your Son to show us the way. Help us keep that childlike wonder throughout our days and remember that like him, we are made in your image.
Amen.

VACATION BIBLE SCHOOL?

Vacation Bible School
Just does not make sense.
Since when is school vacation?
The idea makes me wince.

I've had enough of studying
And sitting still all day
My spelling book and math journal
I want to throw away.

I want to have some fun right now
It can't just be more school
What? VBS has snacks and games?
Now that sounds really cool!

A treasure hunt, a storyteller
Crafts and music, too?
Did I say no to VBS? Well,
I'm going now, aren't you?

*I will instruct you and teach you the way you should go; I
will counsel you with my eye upon you.*
                                          Psalm 32:8

I do think it is funny that this wonderful summertime event put on by so many churches is called *school*. It just seems odd, doesn't it, to have *vacation* and *school* in the same title? And yet, if we remain true to what vacation Bible school is supposed to be, and if school is the place where we learn, then yes, its name is perfect.

We must grab any opportunity we have to teach our children about God and the amazing work of Jesus Christ. It is becoming increasingly harder to protect our children from things we don't think they need to see or be exposed to. Just a walk around the local mall can cause your jaw to drop when you look at your surroundings as a child might. Everything has become so suggestive and in-your-face. Where do we draw the line? What can we do about it?

I say that what we can do is teach our children. Teach them about right and wrong and self-respect. Teach them to care for themselves and others. Help them understand what you consider acceptable and unacceptable. Give them the tools necessary to stay strong and true to themselves. Give them opportunities to strengthen their faith and their belief in themselves. Opportunities like church, time with their family, and of course, vacation Bible school.

Heavenly Father,
Guide us as we make decisions each day. Help us remain true to ourselves and to you.
Amen.

LOST AND FOUND

Mary wasn't the only one
Who lost a little lamb
I learned today in Sunday school
About a shepherd man
He counted sheep to ninety-nine
And found that one had strayed
He searched and searched
To bring it home
That little sheep was saved.

And if he finds it, truly I tell you, he rejoices over it more
than over the ninety-nine that never went astray.
                                        Matthew 18:13

I love the story of the shepherd who goes looking for the lost lamb. What a relief he didn't just say, "Oh well, I've got ninety-nine others. Let's not worry about it."

Think of the real-life examples of shepherds we have in our lives every day. The teacher who reaches out to the child who is struggling in class—though she has twenty-three other students who need her attention, and it would be just as easy to let him slip through the cracks, she doesn't. Or what about the parent who notices his child is acting different and instead of ignoring it as a "teen" thing, takes the time to talk with his child and helps get her back on the right track? Thank goodness for the countless volunteers at homeless shelters who open their hearts and their arms to help those with nowhere else to go.

When Jesus shared this parable, he helped us understand that God will not leave us behind. God is always seeking a relationship with us. Even when we stray, God does not give up on us, but continues reaching out to us.

Gracious and loving God,
You hold us close even when we think we can do it on our own. Thank you for believing in us and loving us no matter where we may go.
Amen.

LOVE ONE ANOTHER

"Love one another"
That's what he said
Sometimes I think
We should tattoo it to our heads.

He said to him, "'You shall love the Lord your God with all your heart, and with all your soul, and with all your mind.' This is the greatest and first commandment. And a second is like it: 'You shall love your neighbor as yourself.'"
Matthew 22:37-39

What is it that is so hard about simply loving one another? Jesus loved everyone. It didn't matter who they were, what they were, or where they came from—he simply loved them and helped them. Even with his great example, we continue to struggle to simply love one another.

The other night we were sitting at a soccer game, one of several that week, and one of the parents had a baby with her. The baby has recently started walking and she was on the move. She would take a few steps, suddenly fall, laugh, and then get right back up to keep exploring. As I watched her roam around, I was touched by how genuinely happy she was to see every person she ran into whether she knew them or not. Her entire face would break out into a

64

huge smile, and she would put her little hand on that person's knee just gazing in pleasure at them. She didn't care what they looked like, what they did for a living, or what they had on. She was simply happy to see them.

Can you imagine going through your day like that? Genuinely happy to see every person you came in contact with. Looking at others as Jesus would, knowing that we are all children of God, worthy of love. Try it. It might be a challenge, but it will certainly be worth it.

Loving God,
Thank you for the example of your Son, who teaches us all what it means to love one another. Help open our eyes to those around us and help us to reach out to them with love. Amen.

GOING UP FRONT

Right before the final note
I jump up ready to go
I have to hurry to get there first
You really can't walk slow

The seat right next to our pastor
Is the one we all race to get
If you're the one that gets there first
You get the very best place to sit.

Our pastor will tell us a story
And he will make us laugh
But the best part of the children's sermon
Is that it's like the fifty-yard dash.

*I call upon you, O LORD; come quickly to me; give ear to my
voice when I call to you.*

Psalm 141:1

I love children's sermon time at church. One of my
children is like a racehorse at the gate just waiting for the
first note of the hymn that is her signal that it is time to
go. From all over the church children are heading up
front to hear a sermon written just for them. You can see
smiles spread across the faces of the congregation watching
this precious procession. You see the perfectly manicured

children in their Sunday best and wonder how their mothers do it. You see the children who look like they just rolled out of bed and feel relief. Some children are dragging little brothers or sisters behind them. And there are always a few children who just sort of saunter up to the front. They take their time, not really in a hurry, but are enjoying the chance to get up and move around during the service.

I am so thankful that our church has a children's sermon. What a wonderful way to say to the children, "We want you here." The children are getting the message that they are an important part of the church family, and we get a chance to see the next generation of our church.

Loving God,
Thank you for the gift of your Word and for the opportunities to share it with our children. Keep their hearts and minds open as they learn your Word.
Amen.

GOD WINKED AT ME

I got back from vacation with a story
For my friends in Sunday school
This is what I told them
It was really, really cool.

I was sitting in the airplane
I got the window seat
I was feeling kind of bored
Sitting there swinging my feet

I was looking out the window
At all the clouds passing by
When suddenly out of nowhere
A silver flash caught my eye

I pressed my nose against the glass
And stared at the ground below
And all of a sudden it flashed again
It thrilled me to my toes

I saw six more silver flashes
Then more clouds came and I couldn't see
My teacher said it was just a reflection
But I know it was God winking at me.

Thanks be to God for his indescribable gift!
2 Corinthians 9:15

Don't you just want to be in that Sunday school classroom to stop that teacher from saying that? So often our children see God in ways we can't even imagine.

What happens to us as we grow older? Why is it more difficult to see God in the simple things around us? Sometimes it seems so hard to be close to God, especially in difficult times. But as the child in this story reminds us, God is always there. Loving us, supporting us, surprising us. Slow down today. Take time to look for the surprises God has in store for you and for your little ones. There are reminders of God's love everywhere just waiting to be seen.

Dear God,
Thank you for the daily reminders you give us that tell us you are always near. Help us learn to slow down so that we may see you and hear you.
Amen.

THE GREAT ESCAPE

I heard the coolest story today
About these guys named Silas and Paul
They'd been beaten up and thrown in jail
But they weren't worried at all.

They just sat there singing
And saying a prayer or two
Then the floors and walls began to shake
And it was "you know who."

The prison doors flew open
And they could have run away
But they just kept on sitting there
For they had much, much more to say.

You see they could have gotten sad
When everything went wrong
But they chose faith and gratitude
And God was with them all along.

They answered, "Believe on the Lord Jesus, and you will be saved, you and your household."
                                    Acts 16:31

Ever had one of those days? One of those days when everything just goes wrong? It is easy to let hardships bring us down, and the lower we get, the more likely we are to strike out at those around us.

But consider the story of Paul and Silas. Talk about not letting the bad things get you down. What a great story to remind us not to let our troubles get the best of us. Together Paul and Silas demonstrated such complete faith that everything would be okay. Even if they couldn't be sure of the outcome, they held on to their faith in God and worshiped God with songs and prayers.

What an important lesson for us to teach our children. It is up to us to decide how we will let hard times affect us. Do we let the hard times beat us down, or do we face the challenges with faith and grace and in the end become stronger? I say choose faith. With God by your side, things will get better and so will you.

Dear Lord,
In the troubled moments of our lives, when things just aren't going our way, help us to hold on to our faith in you and trust that you are with us at that very moment supporting us and loving us.
Amen.

WELCOME TO THE FAMILY

I don't know what just happened
I was simply lying there
When all of sudden
There was water and
It was everywhere
The next thing I knew
I got a kiss
And was lifted way up high
I heard the ahhs and clapping
But I sure didn't know why
I was getting kind of nervous
And I was just about to cry
When my mom showed up real teary
And took me from some guy
Boy was I glad to see her
Because I was ready to go home
I just have one little question
Where did all that water come from?

There is one body and one Spirit, just as you were called to the one hope of your calling, one Lord, one faith, one baptism, one God and Father of all, who is above all and through all and in all.

Ephesians 4:4-6

I always wonder what must go through the minds of babies when they are baptized. One minute they are resting in their mother or father's arms, perhaps enjoying a nice pacifier, when suddenly the pacifier is plucked out and they are handed to a stranger. Then, on top of that, water on the head! No wonder some of them just don't take it that well.

Thank goodness we are there to witness this beautiful moment when a child becomes a member of our Christian family. I always hope that the parents are able to truly be in that moment. It is so easy to get caught up in the other concerns of that special day. We worry about the baby spitting up on the gown, whether or not all the relatives make it in. We worry about the lunch reservations. We hope our baby isn't the one who cries or yells when the water is poured on his or her head.

All these worries and yet, there is one thing we don't have to worry about on the day our child is baptized—and that is God's love for our child and God's love for us.

Gracious God,
Thank you for welcoming us into your family and for
surrounding us with your love.
Amen.

THE LORD'S PRAYER AND OTHER THOUGHTS BY MY LITTLE BROTHER

Our Father
> *(My dad's right here.)*

Who art in Heaven
> *(They do art in Heaven?)*

Hallowed be thy name
> *(What's hollow?)*

Thy Kingdom come
> *(Does God live in a castle?)*

Thy will be done
> *(What's a will?)*

On earth as it is in Heaven
> *(Can I play in Heaven?)*

Give us this day
> *(How do you give a day?)*

Our daily bread
> *(I'm hungry.)*

And forgive us our trespasses
> *(That means don't walk on the grass.)*

As we forgive those who trespass against us.
(My friend stepped on the grass once.)

Lead us not into temptation
(Temptation is a long word.)

But deliver us from evil
(Uh oh. Scary.)

For thine is the kingdom
(Ooh, the castle again.)

and the power
(like Superman?)

and the glory forever and ever
(That sure is a long time.)

Amen.
(Amen.)

He said to them, "When you pray, say . . . "
Luke 11:2

Long before Oprah was famous and shared her "aha" moments, I had my own one summer at camp. It was on a Sunday morning, and the entire camp was on the waterfront for devotional time. After singing a few songs we settled down for a story. One of the counselors was dressed up like a little girl who was preparing to say her prayers. As soon as she said, "Our father," a voice came out of nowhere and said, "Yes?" We all looked around and wondered where the voice came from. The counselor pretending to be the little girl just said, "Shhh, I'm saying my prayers" and started again. After each line of the prayer, "the voice" would ask her a question about her prayer and soon we realized the voice was supposed to be God talking to her. (Of course it was really another counselor hidden behind a tree with a microphone, but the effect was awesome!) As the skit went on we realized that she knew the prayer, but didn't really know what it meant. "God" kept having to explain it to her.

Right at that moment I knew. I knew that even though I had said this prayer at bedtime my whole life, it had never really occurred to me exactly what I was saying. I just knew it was something I should do. What a moment! In one short skit I had all the explanation I needed. I was suddenly asking myself, "Do I really forgive those who 'trespass' against me? Have I thought about the actions I need to be forgiven for? Was I really talking to God or just at God?" That was a significant moment in my prayer life. I finally got it. Let's not forget that we need to make sure our children "get it," too.

Lord,
Your Son gave us the words to bring us closer to you. Help us understand them in our minds and in our hearts.
Amen.

My Tummy Talked in Church Today

SO MANY ANIMALS

Sheep and lions,
Snakes and donkeys,
There's even a big whale, too.
Sometimes the Bible sounds just like
Our field trip to the zoo.

Pairs of all creatures that have the breath of life in them came to Noah and entered the ark.
                                              Genesis 7:15 (NIV)

If you ask most children what stories they know from the Bible, chances are they will immediately come up with the story of Noah's ark. Why is that? What is it about that story that sticks with them?

To me it seems fairly obvious. Soon after most children are born, they receive the first of many stuffed animals. It may be a cuddly bear, a puppy dog, a floppy bunny. We read them books about animals and teach them to make animal sounds. There is nothing cuter than a two-year-old roaring like a lion or mooing like a cow. And if they actually have a pet in the house, that is who they are nose-to-nose with for the first few years of their life. And then when you add trips to the zoo to their animal experience, it becomes obvious why children love that story. It becomes real for them. They can hardly believe Noah was actually on a boat with a giraffe or a monkey. A few worry about tigers being on board and a few wonder if the monkeys made a mess like they do at the zoo.

Children are fascinated with Noah's ark because they can relate to it. They know what animals are. They have seen things that were actually there with Noah. They open their eyes wide, listen intently, and believe. What a gift! To be able to understand something so easily. To connect in a real way.

Dear Heavenly Father,
Each day is a new opportunity to view our world through the eyes of a child. Continue to show us ways to connect to you. Open our hearts to a deeper understanding of you and your grace.
Amen.

My Tummy Talked in Church Today

THE BIG 10

There are ten big rules
Right in that book
They're ones we all should know
I've heard that if you follow them
Your faith will really grow
I get the ones that say don't steal,
And honor your dad and mother…
I'm just glad one doesn't say
To hug your little brother.

Then God spoke all these words: I am the LORD your God.
Exodus 20:1-2

I wonder if God ever thought we would have so much trouble following the Ten Commandments. Every day that I read the paper or watch the news, I am astonished by the number of murders, burglaries, and just plain old meanness that happens in the world. Even people who profess a belief in God are just as likely to break one of the big ten. We hear and see it every day.

Can you imagine how busy God would be if God gave a ticket every time a commandment was broken?

So how do we teach our children that these commandments are truly God's Word and are meant to be followed? How

82

do we teach them that they are NOT merely suggestions and that you don't just have to follow the easy ones?

We do it by example. If we are married, we stay true to our vows. If we see something our neighbor has and we really want it, we slow down and count the blessings we have in front of us. If we find ourselves so angry with someone we could do the unthinkable, we remember that Jesus taught us it is better to forgive. The Ten Commandments are our rules for living. Like the rules of the classroom or the rules of the road, they are meant to be followed.

Gracious Lord,
You gave us life and the guidelines we need to live the best life we can. Please help us every day to honor your Word and be an example to those around us.
Amen.

IN PRAISE OF DONUTS

sugar sweet
piping hot
boxes and boxes full
donuts are
one of my
favorite things about
going to Sunday School

*How sweet are your words to my taste, sweeter than honey
to my mouth!*

Psalm 119:103

I am almost convinced that my church is single-handedly
keeping the donut shops in the area in business. On any
given Sunday morning, you can walk into any room in the
building and there will be boxes of donuts on the table.
People sign up every week to bring them. The varieties are
many, including donut holes, which seem to be a favorite
with the kids.

I think the reason this is so amazing to me is that I don't
even like donuts. Yes, I know I am probably the only
person in the world who doesn't like them, but as I have
considered the popularity of donuts at church, I have come
to regard them as a symbol. A symbol of comfort. It seems
to me that some people go looking for donuts for the same

reasons most people come to church, looking for comfort. We are comfortable with the familiar, with the rituals, and hopefully with God. We seek comfort in the traditions of our faiths and the fellowship we share with our church family.

So, while I may not share a donut with you, I will certainly share in the comfort.

Loving God,
Thank you for the comfort you give us each day. Help us
hold on to the rituals of our faith and feel the comfort of
your loving arms around us.
Amen.

THROWING ROCKS IS NOT ALLOWED

Throwing rocks is not allowed
It's so against the rules
So imagine my surprise today
When I heard this in Sunday School . . .

There was boy named David
Who was brave but very small
Compared to mean Goliath
Who was over nine feet tall.

Well, David said, "I'm not afraid.
I'll take that giant on."
And with great faith
And one small stone
That big old giant was gone.

Now I know that throwing rocks
Is definitely not allowed.
But way back then
David's faith
Must have really made God proud.

If you have faith the size of a mustard seed, you will say to this mountain, "Move from here to there," and it will move; and nothing will be impossible for you.
Matthew 17:20

86

What an amazing example of faith! What complete trust David must have had in God to take on a giant. Wouldn't it be great if we could face all of our "giants" with such unwavering trust and faith?

As we watch the children in our lives grow, we will see them face challenges that we will not be able to protect them from. We must teach our children right from wrong and empower them to make the right choices when faced with a difficult situation. We must remind them that God is on their side and will give them the strength they need when they need it most. It is our job to teach them that it is not the size of your opponent that matters, but the faith in your fight.

Almighty Father,
Thank you for the strength you give us. Help us empower our children with a faith so strong that they can conquer their own personal Goliaths.
Amen.

FAVORITES

Mrs. Vaughan was my favorite teacher
Mrs. Smith was my second best
I don't remember all that much
When I think about the rest.

I do remember Mr. Scott
He was funny and made us laugh
And Mr. Hall was pretty cool
'Cause he knew all the facts.

Ms. Reed was really, really strict
Her class would never end
The thing that they all taught me though
Was that Jesus is my friend.

You are right, Teacher; you have truly said that "he is one, and besides him there is no other."
Mark 12:32

I love to read the stories of people who give credit to a teacher for making a difference in their lives. Stories of teachers who have encouraged, challenged, motivated and loved their students. Usually these stories are about teachers that students had in elementary, junior high, or high school, but I am sure that there are stories out there

88

about Sunday school teachers who have made a difference, too.

I can just picture a Sunday school teacher welcoming a visitor and making them feel important. I can see a Sunday school teacher sharing her faith and helping the children in her class gain a better understanding of what having Jesus in their lives can mean. How about the teacher who always has just the right craft to go with the lesson so that the children can't wait to share what they have done in Sunday school with their parents?

The amount of acceptance, patience, creativity, and love it takes to be a Sunday school teacher is amazing and sometimes, sadly, they are the last to know just how much they mean to their students. So this Sunday, if you see a Sunday school teacher walking by or busy in their classroom, be sure to stop by and say thank you. Say thank you for everything they give the children of your church. Thank them for making sure that God is one of your child's favorites!

Gracious God,
Thank you for the teachers who share your love and your word with others. Open our hearts and our minds so that we may learn from them.
Amen.

REACHING OUT

I bought a goat for a family of four,
A cow for a family of six,
I brought some cans, a coat, some shoes
And added some toys to the mix
A blanket, a shirt, a radio
And coins for the collection plate
I am trying to make a difference today
Try it. It makes you feel great.

Those who are generous are blessed, for they share their bread with the poor.

Proverbs 22:9

I hope as you are reading this you are sitting in a comfortable chair in the air-conditioned comfort of your home. Or perhaps you are sitting in your car waiting in a carpool line, taking advantage of a quiet moment to catch up. Think about where you are right now. Are you surrounded by the things and people you know and love? Are you going about your daily routine as usual? If you are, take a moment and send a little prayer of thanks to God.

Every day we see images of people in need. We hear stories of families living in cars, people who have lost their homes due to a natural disaster, people whose lives have taken a turn down a dangerous path, and children who are going hungry. We receive pleas in the mail from different charities to help fight disease, to help stop violence, and to give an underprivileged child a chance at a better life. With these constant messages, it can become overwhelming; and perhaps we are unsure of where to begin or of how we can possibly help. But the simple truth is, we must.

God commands us to love one another. God doesn't say "Love those just like you" or "Love one another when it is convenient." God simply says, "Love one another." Every day we have a chance to show our children how we can make a difference in another person's life. A chance to show them that it is not all about writing a check and sending it in, though that is helpful, but rather, it is showing God's love to all those around us. Showing kindness to others, giving that man holding a sign on the corner a bottle of water on a hot day, donating food to a food bank, or serving meals at a shelter. We must teach our children to take a look at all the abundance in their lives and see how they can share it with others. Serving God by serving others—what an important lesson and what an amazing feeling.

Almighty God,
You see the need of those around us. Help us open our eyes,
our hearts, and our hands to those who need our love and
support.
Amen.

I TALKED TO GOD TODAY

I talked to God today
I started with a prayer
I said the one I learned in class
I'd paid attention there.

I said, "Our Father"
Then, "Hallowed be ..."
But then I got off track
My mind began to wander
And I couldn't get it back.

I talked to God about my day
My class, my fish, my game
I even talked about that girl
But I didn't mention her name.

And when I stopped I realized
I hadn't said the prayer
But somehow I still knew
That God was
Listening to me up there.

For the eyes of the Lord are on the righteous, and his ears are open to their prayer.

1 Peter 3:12

One of the most important gifts we can give our children is an introduction to God as someone they can always talk to whenever they want. We must help them understand that there are many ways to pray to God and no one will ever say to them, "You are doing that wrong."

God is so happy just to hear from us each day. Talking to God can be as simple as saying thank you for the beautiful trees in your neighborhood or sharing something that made you sad or happy or scared. Every day we have an opportunity to show the children in our lives how we talk to God ourselves. How wonderful to introduce them to a loving friend who will always be there for them.

Dear Heavenly Father,
Thank you for always being there to hear our triumphs and our woes, our concerns and our successes. Help us always remember to give you thanks for the blessing of each day.
Amen.

HEAVEN ON EARTH

My minister said the words "heaven on earth"
And I've been trying to figure it out
I'm not really sure what he meant by that
So I asked my family to find out.

My grandfather said when I asked him
That his farm was heaven on earth
But then I heard my mom reply
It had been the beach for her since birth.

So I asked around and to my surprise
My uncle said baseball was it.
But my cousin laughed that heaven on earth
Was a day when everything fit.

My great aunt said it was beautiful music
But my sister said it's being outside
The lady next door said laughing with friends
Her little girl said it's going down a slide.

It can be different for everyone asked
This I'm beginning to see
What's your idea of heaven on earth?
Will you share it with me?

In my Father's house are many rooms; if it were not so, I would have told you. I am going there to prepare a place for you.

John 14:2 (NIV)

What a huge idea to wrap our minds around! Children often ask what heaven is like and many adults are stumped when it comes to an answer. Some describe a beautiful scene, some a place in the clouds, and some simply say, "I don't know." I once heard in a movie that it is different for everyone. That makes sense to me.

When I think of Jesus making a room for us, it seems obvious to me that we wouldn't all have the same exact room. God made us all so unique down here that I have to believe that our spirits remain equally unique. It is okay to tell our children that we don't know. But along with that, I would ask them to imagine their favorite place and explain that it might be just like that.

Dear God,
Though we don't know exactly what is to come, we take comfort in knowing that you are indeed waiting for us with open arms and everlasting love.
Amen.

SNAKE BIT

I've been doing some thinking
About Adam and Eve
And there's something that just doesn't fit.
Why in the world would you talk to a snake
When everyone knows that you risk getting bit?
And weren't they surprised that the snake spoke at all,
I mean who ever heard of that?
If I saw a snake, much less one that could talk,
I'd be gone in ten seconds flat!
But talk they did and you know the story.
Their lives were never the same.
So let's learn from them and always
Beware of a snake who knows your name.

The serpent tricked me, and I ate.
Genesis 3:13

How easy it is for us to be tricked or talked into doing something we shouldn't. Even as adults we can sometimes have trouble deciding if a person is genuine or not. And what an awful feeling when we realize someone we believed in or trusted is not what they seem.

From the very beginning we teach our children about "stranger danger" and what to do if someone they don't

96

know approaches them. And yet, we constantly hear of yet another child who is missing or in harm's way, lured away by the supposed kindness of a stranger.

Just as Eve was tempted by the promises of how great it would be to know good and evil like God, our children can be tempted by promises of candy, a puppy, anything that appeals to them and their sense of fun. One of the beautiful things about children is how trusting they are; and the question is how we teach them to be wary and safe without extinguishing that trusting nature.

I wish I had an easy answer for that, but I will simply say that we must continue to educate without scaring, protect without smothering, and most of all be there for the children in our lives. We may not be able to keep them away from all the "snakes" in their paths, but we can certainly continue to love and support them when they meet one.

Dear God,
As we travel life's path, please help us keep our eyes open and focused on you and your great love. Give us strength to face the snakes in our paths.
Amen.

THE BALCONY

I sat up in the balcony today
I've never been up there
I told my mom I couldn't breathe
I'm sure it was thin air

I couldn't see the minister
Or really anything
The acolytes were miniscule
The choir looked like ants who sing

I looked around and saw some folks
Who'd sat up here before
With squinty eyes they surveyed the church
But they could see no more

My ears were stretched, I tried my best
But still I couldn't hear
It felt like we had been in church
Almost an entire year.

So lesson learned, now I know
The balcony's not that great.
I guess now I'll get up on time
To make sure we're not late.

For everything there is a season, and a time for every matter under heaven.

Ecclesiastes 3:1

My Tummy Talked in Church Today

Ron Benedict

Why is it so hard to wake up in the morning? There are days when I can hardly drag myself out of bed. And yet, there are some days when I hop right up with a smile on my face, ready to go. On those days, there is usually something I am really looking forward to doing. Maybe meeting an old friend for lunch or going to see a new movie or simply getting to stay home with no agenda or to-do list.

Recently a friend shared with me that she had to get up earlier than usual one Saturday, and though she considers Saturday her only day to "sleep in" and wasn't thrilled about getting up, she ended up having one of the best mornings. She got to enjoy a peaceful walk in the cool morning air and have some quiet time to herself. She found herself pleasantly surprised at what the morning had meant to her.

Don't you wish every morning could be like that? If you think about it, there is at least one day a week when we should all be excited to get up. Each Sunday we have the opportunity to join our family and friends in giving thanks and worshiping God together. It is our chance to feel a part of a collective whole as we remember each day is truly a gift from God, and it is up to us to make the most of each one. So talk to your children about what you love about Sunday mornings and how you can make them even more special. Next Sunday, you might find you don't even need an alarm clock!

Loving and precious God,
Thank you for the gift of each day and the opportunity to share it with others. Amen.

My Tummy Talked in Church Today

THE BLUE ROBE

If I mouth the words
Do they know
I don't know how to sing?

If I close my eyes
And open wide
Will they suspect a thing?

You see I love this bright blue robe
The choir wears to sing
But I can't hit a single note ...
I just want to wear this thing.

My servants shall sing for gladness of heart.
Isaiah 65:14

I love to sit and listen to a choir sing. I love to close my eyes and listen to the beautiful sounds their voices make as they blend together bringing hymns to life. I love how they look in their robes and how they fill the chancel. They look like one giant gift about to be opened.

To me it is one of the greatest gifts to be able to sing. Let me be quick to tell you, I did not get that gift! As much as I like to belt songs out in my car, I know that I can't hit a note and that truthfully it would be painful if anyone had to actually hear me. Currently my children still ask me to sing to them at bedtime, but it is only a matter of time before they stop asking.

I vividly remember begging my mom not to sing in church because she was so off-key. In true preteen fashion, I would get so embarrassed and tug on her arm hissing, "Please stop." She would just look at me and laugh and keep on singing. My mom knew. My mom knew that God did not care what her voice sounded like. My mom knew that going to church was her time to offer herself to God, and she wasn't worried about what anyone thought. She fully participated in every aspect of the service and she sang the songs with gusto. What a role model.

I see now that I should have been proud, impressed even, that my mom knew what really matters. Not your singing voice, not your pretty clothes, not even how much money you put in the plate. What matters most is what is in our hearts and that we offer ourselves to God freely without reservation. So if you, like me, tend to mouth the words in church, take a chance this Sunday and sing with all your heart. Be an example to the children around you of what worship is really all about.

Loving God,
Thank you for accepting us as we are. As we lift our voices to you, help us remember that it is not the sound of our voices, but the love in our hearts that truly matters. Amen.

My Tummy Talked in Church Today

FOLLOWING THE LEADER

Follow the leader is the name of the game
That I really like to play
But I heard a whole new version of it
In Sunday school today.

You see these guys were fishing
They did it every day
When Jesus came on walking by
And said, "Follow me this way."

Can you believe they stopped right there
And left their boats on shore
They left it all to follow him
Their leader and Savior.

*Lead me in your truth, and teach me, for you are the God
of my salvation; for you I wait all day long.*
Psalm 25:5

"Your child is a natural-born leader." This was said to my
husband and me once at a parent-teacher conference. Of
course, I immediately took this as a huge compliment and
sat up a bit straighter ready to hear more about my child.
(At moments like these my husband likes to remind me
she is "our" child.)

As we listened more to what her teacher had to say, it became clear that even though this was good news, it also came with a healthy dose of responsibility. How could we as parents make sure that our daughter was leading her friends down the path of good and not trouble? Both paths have leaders and you can just turn on the news to hear about leaders who steer people the wrong direction. How could we be sure to encourage good decision-making and secure her knowledge of right from wrong?

One thing was clear. We could not do it alone. We would need the support of our family, our friends, and of course, our church. Each week as we pick up our child from Sunday school or sit in the sanctuary as a family, I know that our children are hearing and seeing wonderful examples of goodness and faith. I pray that these messages become a part of who they are and guide them on their path.

Gracious God,
We thank you for being a guiding light to us as we travel on our paths. Help us make good decisions and responsible choices and continue to look to the example of your Son, Jesus Christ.
Amen.

My Tummy Talked in Church Today

WAKE UP!

I have to keep my eyes wide open
Though I've been up since dawn
One thousand eyes are on me
Mom will kill me if I yawn
Just one more song
And one more prayer
And then we're finally through
Being an acolyte is really tough
When everyone's looking at you.

Only fear the LORD, and serve him faithfully with all your heart; for consider what great things he has done for you.
1 Samuel 12:24

Every once in a while during church my husband will nudge me and tell me to watch. I know what he really means is "Check out the acolyte, he's going down." Sometimes we can't help getting the giggles watching some of these kids fighting so hard to keep their eyes open or trying to stifle yawn after yawn. Once there was even one young man who totally lost the battle. His head was leaning all the way back and his mouth was wide open as he caught a quick snooze. Finally the other acolyte gave him an elbow to the ribs and he woke up. All I could think about was his mom, somewhere out there in the

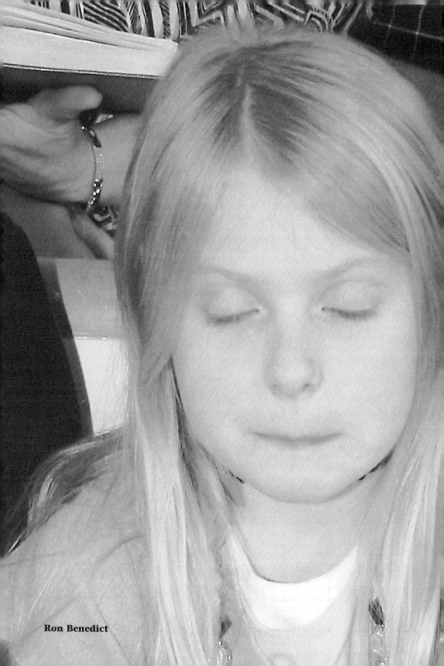

Ron Benedict

congregation, trying to send telepathic messages to him to "WAKE UP!" I am sure he got an earful later.

I have to say, though, I am always impressed with the kids who join the acolyte team. They are truly putting themselves out there in front of everyone. They are practicing their faith openly in front of their peers. The adolescent and young adult years can be tough. At a time when fitting in and being the "same" as everyone else is high on the priority list, it is comforting to see teens who also keep their faith high on the list. So let's give these kids a hand. The next time you have a chance to speak to an acolyte, be sure to let them know you appreciate what they do. Thank them for being good role models for the younger children in the church. And thank them for helping you remember to keep your faith high on the list, too.

Lord,
Every day we have an opportunity to thank you, praise you,
and keep you high on the list. Thank you for the examples
of faith you put in our lives every day.
Amen.

SWALLOWED!

Jonah made a choice one day
That wasn't really good
So he ended up inside a whale
Until he understood
That listening to God
Is something that we all must do
Because if you don't, that is when
Something big could swallow you!

*Do not fear, for I am with you, do not be afraid, for I am
your God; I will strengthen you, I will help you, I will
uphold you with my victorious right hand.*
                                        Isaiah 41:10

Sometimes in our lives things happen that do indeed seem
to swallow us whole. It could be a death in the family, an
illness, an argument with a loved one, financial difficulties,
or any number of things. We find ourselves consumed with
the issue and sometimes it can be truly overwhelming with
seemingly no end in sight. And, while we have these huge
issues on our hearts, we still have to continue on with our
day-to-day lives. Carpools must be driven, meals must be
cooked, laundry must be washed, jobs must be done, and
families must be cared for. The question is how do we do
it? Where will we get the strength we need? How do we
take care of ourselves and our children?

My Tummy Talked in Church Today

This is the time when we must truly rely on our faith. As hard as it may be, we must remember that God is with us and these feelings of uncertainty, sadness, fear, loneliness, or isolation will eventually lessen. We have to remember that when we are going through something like this, the children in our lives are still looking to us for love, guidance, and reassurance that everything will be okay. The issue may be beyond their comprehension, but children always know when something is going on. So what do we do? We trust God.

We have faith. We take each day one at a time. When we feel as if we have been swallowed whole, we must show our children how we rely on our faith in God to see us through.

Gracious God,
Thank you for supporting us in our times of need and giving us the strength we need to get through each day. Amen.

NOAH'S PUDDING

Brown and mushy
Spicy or sweet
A gesture of friendship
A historical treat
It reminds us all
From Noah we came
In the eyes of God
We are all the same.

God said, "This is the sign of the covenant that I make between me and you and every living creature that is with you, for all future generations."
Genesis 9:12

I would love to go into a room and ask for a show of hands of how many people have heard of Noah's pudding. Up until a year ago, I had never heard of it. That all changed due to a visitor at our church. For several months a young man of the Muslim faith visited our church and attended services each Sunday. He developed a friendship with our senior pastor and said he felt welcome and enjoyed learning more about the Christian faith. One Sunday he asked if he could share one of his faith's traditions with the congregation to say thank you. He shared with us Noah's pudding.

According to the Institute of Interfaith Dialogue, Noah's pudding is made each year following the Islamic calendar to celebrate the landing of Noah's Ark. It symbolizes the essential unity of human beings and their relationship to one another and to God. It is a tradition that helps people maintain good relations with their neighbors whatever their religion or beliefs may be. Preparing Noah's pudding is a common practice among both Muslims and Christians throughout the Mediterranean area.

It was such a cool experience to see this young man and his friends offering us individual servings of Noah's pudding. The fact that they had gone to the trouble to cook so much of it and share it with us in a true gesture of friendship was inspiring. I was so happy my children saw these young men from different backgrounds and a different faith reaching out to us. I can't think of a better reminder that we are all children of God and we are in this together.

Gracious God,
Thank you for the reminder that we are indeed all your children.
Amen.

DON'T FORGET TO SAY THANK YOU

There were ten in all
They were very sick
They simply wanted to get well
They saw Jesus coming and ran to him
Then you could hear them yell.

"Help us, help us"
They all cried out
And Jesus turned their way
"Go now to the temple," he said to the ten.
"Your faith has healed you today."

They heard his words
And off they went
But here the story takes a turn
Only one turned around to say thank you to Jesus
The other nine didn't even return.

What a surprise
That must have been
To see the nine men go
I wonder if Jesus was sad or not
I think probably so.

Give thanks in all circumstances, for this is God's will for you in Christ Jesus.

1 Thessalonians 5:18 (NIV)

My Tummy Talked in Church Today

Several times I have had the opportunity to be a part of a chapel service at a nearby elementary school. My part was to tell a story related to their theme of the month. One day I was walking out with the children as they were leaving and suddenly I heard a little voice say, "Thank you." I turned to see a young man who was walking behind me. He smiled at me and again said, "Thank you."

Thank you. Two simple words. Thank you. Two simple words that can make a difference in your whole day. I was amazed at the power of these two words. I instantly felt a smile come over my face and was so pleased he had enjoyed my story. As more people came up to me and said thank you, that positive feeling grew and grew. In fact, it was with me all day.

I tell you this because every day we have the opportunity to say thank you. Not only to God, for our many, many blessings, but also to our spouses, our children, their teachers, our co-workers, the person at the drive-thru window, and countless others. Those two simple words that let others know we are grateful for them and appreciate their time, their attention, their service, their love; two simple words that can make the difference in a person's day. Don't miss any opportunity today to say, "Thank you!" You'll be so glad you did!

Dear God,
Thank you, thank you, thank you.
Amen.

GOD, ARE YOU THERE?

Now I lay me down to sleep
Hoping I won't hear a creak
I'm hoping God will stay nearby
I'm trying real hard not to cry.

The sitter's in the other room
My parents left today at noon
I say my prayers most every night
But without them here, it's just not right.

Mom always says, don't be scared
Just say your prayer and you're prepared
For a nice long sleep all through the night
God will be with you until first light.

I hope so. . . . Good night!

When you lie down, you will not be afraid; when you lie down, your sleep will be sweet.
Proverbs 3:24 (NIV)

When I was a little girl I somehow got it into my head that once you said your prayers at night you couldn't open your eyes again until morning. If you did, you had to say your prayers all over again. As a result of this self-imposed rule, I would end up saying the Lord's Prayer anywhere from three to twenty times a night depending on when I finally fell asleep.

I still remember the night I told my dad about it. Mom was out of town and he was sitting with me while I said my prayers. When I finished, I explained my frustration with the whole thing. I wondered if God got tired of hearing me over and over again. How my dad held back the laughter is still a mystery to me, but he looked me in my seven-year-old eyes and explained that it really wasn't a rule and God understood all about not being able to keep your eyes closed. He said God is just happy to hear from you, and saying your prayers once at bedtime is plenty. What a relief! I'm sure I slept much better that night.

The good news was that no matter how many times I said my prayers, I never lost the feeling that God was really right there with me in my room. I felt safe and loved and protected no matter how many times I ended up having to say my prayers. As an adult, I still feel the same way. I hope my girls and the children in your life feel the same way each night as they say their prayers. I hope they truly understand that God is listening and is with them.

Lord,
Your presence is a comfort in our lives. Thank you for your love and protection.
Amen.

1, 2, MARY KNEW

1, 2, Mary knew
3, 4, Joseph adored
5, 6, Bed of hay and sticks
7, 8, Shepherds wait
9, 10, The story begins. . . .

In a loud voice she exclaimed: "Blessed are you among women, and blessed is the child you will bear!"
Luke 1:42 (NIV)

The holidays are here! And along with that comes the hustle and bustle of the season, making list after list of things to do, things to buy, and people to see. It is easy to get caught up in those lists and lose sight of the real meaning of Christmas. If we only had time to consider what Christmas means to us and what we want it to mean to our children! When I think about Mary and Joseph's journey to Bethlehem, I realize that they had time. Time to reflect on their lives and what lay ahead. Imagine their thoughts and plans knowing that God had chosen them to be the parents of God's Son.

We have been chosen as well. We have been given one of the greatest gifts imaginable, our children. This year try to make the month of December your own journey to

Ron Benedict

Christmas. Get out a calendar and plan special days for you and your children. It doesn't have to be grand—a simple cup of hot chocolate and reading their favorite stories one afternoon or picking out the perfect tree as a family. Pick a day to put on Christmas music and wrap presents together. Read the story of Jesus' birth in the Bible one night. Put these events on the calendar and give your children and yourself something to look forward to in the hectic weeks ahead. Time to reflect and time together. That's all they really want anyway.

Dear Lord,
Thank you for those special moments that will stay with us as memories throughout our lives. Help us take the time to reflect on each day, remembering your gifts of grace and goodness.
Amen.

HOW WISE WERE THE WISE MEN?

How wise were the wise men
As they followed that bright star?
How faithful were the shepherds
As they came from near and far?
How sure were Mary and Joseph
Of the gift they had to bring?
They all knew of God's great love
When they heard the angels sing.

But the angel said to them, "Do not be afraid; for see—I am
bringing you good news of great joy for all the people."
Luke 2:10

What would happen today if someone came up to you
and said, "See that baby over there? He will be king and
has come to save us." Seriously, how would you react? I
can think of a million reactions and truly not one of them
is of a person walking over to the baby and kneeling to
pray confident they have met the Son of God.

And yet, Mary, Joseph, the shepherds, and the wise men
did just that. Mary, a young girl, suddenly filled with the
Holy Spirit and responsible for so much, and Joseph,
steadfast in his devotion to Mary when so many others
must have scoffed, simply accepted this blessing. We hear

about the shepherds being told by angels and the wise men getting word, and yet not a one of them said, "Well, let me think about it. Are you sure? How do you know this is true?" They simply believed and journeyed to see the king.

When I was growing up my mother used to say, "Don't believe anything you hear and only half of what you see." I have even caught myself saying it to my girls. It has always seemed like good advice; that we can't know the whole story by only hearing or seeing bits and pieces of it; find out the truth yourself.

And yet, Mary, Joseph, the shepherds, and the wise men did just that. No questions asked. They knew not only in their minds, but also in their hearts that it was true. The Son of God was here. Rejoice!

Giving God,
We can only hope to have the strength of Mary and Joseph, the faith of the shepherds, and the wisdom of the wise men. Thank you for their example and thank you for the gift of your Son.
Amen.

Ron Benedict

USHERS

The ushers show me
Where to go
A place they'll help me find
It's amazing that on
Christmas Eve
They don't all lose their minds.

Of this gospel I have become a servant according to the gift of God's grace that was given me by the working of his power.
Ephesians 3:7

Sometimes they are the first people you see when you arrive. They put themselves out there to be the greeters of the church. They welcome members and visitors, pass out the bulletins, collect the offering, find that last seat, and keep things running smoothly. And yet, when was the last time you said thank you to an usher? I am embarrassed to say that I have not done it in a while.

Being an usher is another of those "church" jobs that carries great responsibility and yet is carried out in such a dignified and quiet manner we may not even realize what they face each week. And on Christmas Eve? Wow, the patience they must have to deal with the massive crowds, visitors new to the church and regulars who want "their"

122

pew. I can't imagine it is much fun to explain that saving seats is not allowed. I'm sure it is easy to feel unappreciated at times.

Once again we have a great opportunity to educate our children. We can help them understand that not everything happens at the front of the church; that in every church there are countless volunteers who are behind the scenes making it all happen. Volunteers who help make our experience at church meaningful. Volunteers who could use a little "Merry Christmas," too.

Holy One,
Thank you for those who serve you with loving hearts in our churches.
Amen.

FOLLOWING THE STAR

How did they know
When they saw that star
That it was the one to follow?

How did they know
That the star in the sky
Would lead them to one so holy?

It seems a big risk
A mighty big chance
To follow a star through the night.

But they followed that star
With confidence and trust and
They met our Savior that night.

*Where is the child who has been born king of the Jews? For
we observed his star at its rising, and have come to pay
him homage.*

Matthew 2:2

To me, one of the most beautiful sights in the world is a
clear night sky full of stars. I remember the first time I
went to camp, away from city lights, and saw more stars
than I had ever seen in my life. I remember wanting to see

My Tummy Talked in Church Today

all the constellations so bad, but I was usually only able to pick out the Big and Little Dippers. I still get excited to see the first star of the night, and I still find myself making the wish I made as a child: "Star light, star bright, first star I see tonight, I wish I may, I wish I might, have the wish I wish tonight."

I wonder what the three wise men were wishing that night as they followed the star to Bethlehem. Did they wish for peace? Did they wish for guidance? What were they hoping for? It seems they had everything they needed, and yet they traveled far across the land to find this baby who would be king.

What will you wish for this Christmas season? What do you hope that the year ahead will bring for you and your family? My wish for you is that you have love and faith, strength and happiness, safety and peace.

Merry Christmas!

Loving God,
You know the wishes in our hearts. Help us keep our eyes on the stars and be reminded again and again of the gift you gave each of us.
Amen.

WHO ARE YOU?

When I look at Jesus, I see some of me
I try to love others and hope they love me.

I try to be nice and giving and fair
I try to be patient and I try to share

I try to put others first, I invite friends to play
I try to remember to pray every day

But sometimes it's hard to be just like him
Like when I get mad at someone, that is when ...

I forget all I've learned and I say mean stuff
I shout and I pout and I get in a huff

But that's not really what God wants to see
That's why God sent Jesus, so he could teach me.

*He came to Jesus at night and said, "Rabbi, we know you
are a teacher who has come from God. For no one could
perform the miraculous signs you are doing if God were not
with him."*

John 3:2 (NIV)

126

I was sitting at a red light the other day listening to the radio. One of the songs I heard has been stuck in my head for days. The words of that song have me thinking. Am I the person I want to be? Can I actually be that person, and what does she look like? I know I will not magically grow any taller any time soon, nor will the wrinkles I have earned go away, and I'm fairly certain I won't suddenly start liking exercise anytime soon. But it occurred to me that the answer is not so much about what I look like on the outside as who I am on the inside. Am I the kind of person I want my children to look to as a role model? Do I smile more than frown? Do I support more than tear down? Am I an optimist or a pessimist? Do I practice my faith or just go through the motions? Am I loving and giving or selfish and jealous? Tough questions!

As I continued thinking about the person I am and want to be, it dawned on me that the next logical question is am I the person God wants me to be? God sent us the perfect example of who God wants us to be in God's Son, Jesus Christ. Compassionate, caring, generous. God does not want us to be judgmental or selfish, but rather wants us to be giving of ourselves and our love. We merely have to follow Jesus' example. So, as we head into a new year I want to wish you and your family many blessings, and may we all be the people God wants us to be.

Gracious God,
Thank you for sending your Son to teach us how to be the people you want us to be. Amen.

My Tummy Talked in Church Today